T0121088

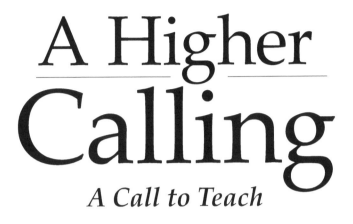

A Higher Calling

A Call to Teach

SCOTT PETZNICK

WESTBOW
P R E S S®
A DIVISION OF THOMAS NELSON
& ZONDERVAN

WestBow Press books may be ordered through booksellers or by contacting:

WestBow Press
A Division of Thomas Nelson & Zondervan
1663 Liberty Drive
Bloomington, IN 47403
www.westbowpress.com
844-714-3454

ISBN: 978-1-6642-4270-8 (sc)
ISBN: 978-1-6642-4271-5 (e)

Library of Congress Control Number: 2021916354

Print information available on the last page.

WestBow Press rev. date: 9/7/2021

Dedication

This book is dedicated to my mother. She owned every Harlequin Romance novel written to man. Being a voracious reader and educator, she instilled in me the love of education and the joy of reading. I wish she could have been here to see the publication of this book, but I know that she would have been proud. Love you, Mom!

Introduction

"If I had only known that before I started teaching!" I can't tell you how many times I have said that to myself. It would have prevented many of the potholes that I have stepped into during the twenty-plus years of my teaching career. Teaching is really like parenting; by the time you start to figure out what is going on and what to do, it's over.

This is a book I have started so many times, sometimes on paper and hundreds of times in my head. It seems that as each year comes and goes, I am mentally adding new chapters to this book. Like most people, many of us have dreams and bucket lists that we want to try or accomplish in our lives. For me, this is one of those items. This is not a scientific book based on a lot of research and footnotes. Rather, this is a book that captures a few of the lessons and stories that I have learned and gone through during my over two decades of teaching. I don't profess to have all the answers—or any answers frankly—but I will share some insights that I have learned over the years, And I will ask some very pointed questions to get you, the reader, to think about your teaching.

Some may use this as a devotional book or a supplemental college textbook. A PLC (personal learning community) may even use some chapters as part of their teacher in-service training programs. You might be just thinking about becoming a teacher; maybe you are in a college teaching program or have been teaching for years. No matter what stage you are at in teaching, it is always good to step back and ask yourself the bigger questions about teaching. Things like: Why do I want to teach? What is my motivation to teach? What part of teaching is the most important? What are my students getting in my classroom? What am I getting from the students? These are just a few questions teachers really need to ask themselves each and every day. Why? To answer that, let me introduce you to student teacher X.

This student teacher was working in a sixth-grade classroom as an intern. There was no real supervising teacher over them, so they were on their own. Unfortunately, that was a tough year to be teaching sixth grade. The hormones were raging and there had developed a major division between the girls. The girls were divided into two main groups, with a couple of girls abstaining from the catfight. It had finally come to a raging boil before Christmas, and the student teacher was at their wit's end.

One day one of the boys in their class was inside for noon recess, helping with some stuff in the classroom. The student teacher came and sat by him with a concerned look on his face. "What am I going to do about the girl situation that has developed?" the student teacher asked. Engraved on the face of the student teacher was a concerned, hurt, worried expression. The student teacher was a great person and well liked as a teacher but had absolutely no classroom management skills.

The catfight was never resolved, and mercifully, the semester came to an end. After that semester, the student teacher went on to have a very successful career in real estate. The student teacher was not meant to be a teacher. Somewhere along the path they missed a few important questions, and when reality set in, it was culture shock. The student teacher would never recover from that experience and turned to real estate as a profession. And it was a far better fit.

My purpose for this book is to challenge you to think about some of the bigger-picture questions and maybe help you to refine your thoughts and reasons for why and how you teach. My hope is that this book will inspire you as a teacher or maybe show you that teaching might not be the best profession for you. Either way, I hope you will take these principles and apply them to whatever occupation you are in because I think they are universal in their applications.

A Higher Calling

Not many of you should become teachers,
my brothers, for you know that we who teach
will be judged with greater strictness.

—JAMES 3:1 (ESV)

Why does one become a teacher? Is it because of the influence of an inspiring teacher in one's life? Possibly someone wanting to make a difference in a child's life? Maybe it was because someone came from a long line of teachers, and it was expected that they would join the profession. Could it be that they were undecided in college, and their parents forced them to pick something because they were going to cut off the funding, so they chose teaching? Oh, we can't forget those who wanted summers off so they could have the freedom to hunt, fish, vacation, or do any other activity. Regardless of the reasons, many of us have become teachers, for better or worse. Does the reason someone becomes a teacher matter?

I would like you to consider the reason why you chose to teach. It matters to your students. Your motivation for being in a classroom drastically affects your students, their parents, and your coworkers. I truly believe that teaching is a higher calling, and a teacher's influence goes way beyond learning time tables or how to read. Teachers can impact students in good or bad ways. I will be giving many examples to prove my points, and I want you to be thinking about the bigger picture as we go through this book.

I can't tell you what educational lessons I learned on any particular day in my third-grade class, but I can tell you that I loved that teacher because of the way the teacher made each of us feel special, their sense of humor, and the way the teacher read books aloud. If you were to poll my elementary classmates on who was the best teacher, this teacher would win hands down. You see, the impact that a teacher makes is less about the learning and more about the relationship.

I can still remember the email I received from a student I had my first year of teaching. I had graduated college midyear and took on a long-term sub position in third grade. It was a rough class, but one of the students I had that year contacted me through my school email when she was a senior and had just moved to the district where I was currently teaching. She wanted to let me know that I had inspired her. She also said she remembered all the songs I taught them that year in third grade and that I was her favorite teacher. I have received many emails and Facebook messages over the years from students expressing the impact that I made on their lives. I am sure that most of those students cannot remember any of the lessons I taught them. What they do remember are my interactions with them, the relationships I had with them!

So why did I become a teacher? I guess my answer would be that I was born to teach. It was in my genetics. How do I know? Well, for me it started when I was a kindergartener. I remember riding the little yellow school bus home from school. I grew up on a dairy farm nine miles out of town, so the bus ride was forty-five minutes long, which seemed like an eternity for a kindergartener. Jumping off the bus, I would race to my playhouse. My playhouse was an old, run-down farmhouse that was the original farmhouse for the farm. We had built a new house, and they hadn't demolished the old house yet, so naturally I took ownership of the house, and it became my playhouse. I would run upstairs to my old bedroom. My mom was a teacher's aide, so of course my room was furnished with a chalkboard on one wall. The alphabet was spread across the top of the room, just like in most elementary classrooms. Waiting for me to get home was Pooh Bear. He was sitting in an old high chair that I used as a baby. He was always eager and ready to learn. I would open my backpack and pull out all the papers I had done that day. One by one I would go over each lesson and paper with Pooh Bear, just like my teacher had done with me earlier that day. I tried to use the same language my teacher used and would correct Pooh Bear when he drew a letter or number incorrectly. Funny how he made the same mistakes as I had made that day! Little did I know at the time that I was reinforcing all the lessons I had learned by teaching them to Pooh Bear. So as a young child, I had already begun to lay a foundation for becoming a teacher. Instead of playing cars or cops and robbers, I was in my playhouse, reinforcing what I learned at school. More important, I was beginning my journey to becoming a teacher.

As I continued to grow, like many other young boys I dreamed of becoming an astronaut, a doctor, professional basketball player, and a number of other occupations that seemed interesting. But somewhere deep in the back of my mind I could not extinguish the longing to teach, to take what I had learned and pass it on to others and watch the sparks go off in their eyes. That never gets old, by the way! No matter how long I teach, I never tire of seeing the sparks go off in others' eyes as they grasp a new concept. I eventually gave in to my calling, and as someone once said, "If you do what you love, you never work a day in your life."

As we travel through this book together, I want you, as the reader, to reflect on why you chose teaching. How did you feel about teaching when you started, and how do you feel about it now? Would you have changed your decision knowing what you know now? These are things to ponder as we go through this book. Your answers may have a direct impact on your future. My purpose here is to help you understand the *why*. Too many students go into teaching wanting to learn the *how* and completely miss the most important question, why! The final question for this chapter is one we have already alluded to but now it's your turn. Why do you teach or want to teach?

Blank Slate

Remember not the former things, nor consider the things of old. Behold, I am doing a new thing; now it springs forth, do you not perceive it? I will make a way in the wilderness and rivers in the desert.

—ISAIAH 43:18–19 (ESV)

"Do you have a brother?" the teacher asked. "Yes, sir," was my reply. And, reader, that was the beginning of two of the worst years of my educational life. That teacher was the junior high social studies teacher who apparently had a really good memory, or maybe it was that my brother had made such a monumental impression that there was no way I was going to slide under this teacher's radar.

Even though my brother was five years older than I, he had obviously stood out like a giraffe in a muddle of guinea pigs. As with many families, children are different, and while growing up, my brother and I were polar opposites. My brother tended to push the envelope, while I preferred the calmer way of life. Unfortunately, my brother's previous envelope pushing was beginning to rain on my parade, so to speak. His reputation began to affect my GPA seriously. The worst of it for me was in my social studies class.

My social studies teacher looked the part of a teacher. They would wear an ironed, button-up shirt with a tie each day and they would round out the outfit with a nicely pressed pair of dress pants and a pair of loafers. But being a teacher stopped at the looks. My social studies teacher was not a teacher. Most days the students would be alone, reading a social studies book or drawing some map, and the teacher would be making sure we colored in the lines. "Make sure your lines are all going the same direction as you color," they would say. My social studies teacher expected the maps to look perfect. So what was my social studies teacher doing while the students were reading their social studies books or sharpening their colored pencils for the tenth time that day? The teacher was sitting at their desk in the back of the room. Their legs would be propped up on the desk, and the local newspaper would be opened so wide all you could see were a couple tiny fingers holding on to the edges. That's what my teacher did every day. They read the paper from front to back. I guess time goes by fast when you are reading about politics or if your favorite sports teams are predicted to win. Reading the newspaper may have helped my teacher with game-day picks, but it really did not help me to learn social studies.

When my social studies teacher did teach, it was comical at best. They would open the class door, which was in the front of the room, and hug the wall as they spoke. They had one leg inside the classroom and one leg outside the classroom and would straddle the wall like it was their security blanket. Then they would randomly flip the light switch on and off as they spoke. It was totally distracting and a source of many chuckles and giggles. The teacher never seemed to know why their class was giggling all the time. Needless to say, that was how my forty-five minutes of social studies went every day.

I had always been a really good student with very good grades. But since entering this teacher's room, I could not for the life of me get an A. It didn't matter what I did in class, the teacher always made sure that it was no higher than a B+. Why should I be punished for my brother's behavior? I remember going to my mother and complaining about the unfair treatment I was getting. Not wanting to rock the boat, my mother's answer was to just let it go. She would say, "It's only junior high, and it will not be on your permanent records." That was not the answer I was looking for. I wasn't happy with that decision, but what else could I do? I vowed that if I was ever to become a teacher, I would not treat my students this way. I would give each of my students a blank slate.

Because of that school year, when I finally became a teacher, I provided each of my students with a blank slate each year. I didn't care where they came from, who they were related to, what they wore, the color of their skin, or the language they spoke. All children would be given a blank slate each year. Even if I had that same child a second or third year, I always made sure that I gave the benefit of the doubt to each child. This blank slate theory was great until the year I had a student who was a real challenge.

I loved to play the guitar in the classroom. I have songs I use in math and science and some that are just silly and fun. This one particular year I had a challenging student. I was walking into the classroom one day and another student yelled, "Mr. P., Student X broke your guitar!" As I walked over to the back of my desk, where I kept my guitar on its guitar stand, I saw the neck of the guitar was completely broken. The neck was now in the shape of an L. I looked at the student who did it, and he looked at me. I knew in my gut that I had to let this go. I felt the Lord say to me, *You cannot get upset about this.* In my mind I was thinking, *God, do you know how much a guitar costs?* Reluctantly I obeyed the Lord and never said a word to this student. After sending them out to recess, I just gathered up what was left of the guitar and went out and threw it in the Dumpster. I may never know the story behind the broken guitar, and I probably never will, but right then and there, that student needed a blank slate.

But that was not the end of the guitar story. This is where the story really gets good. You see, one of the other students came into class a couple days later and handed me a new guitar. They had been so upset by what happened they went home and asked their mom if they could give me a new guitar that was sitting in the closet of their house. It had never been used and was just collecting dust. Their parents said yes, so the student came bouncing into the classroom the next day carrying their gift, a guitar. I still use it in my classroom today! Some may call it karma or coincidence, but I call it God's blessing. God had already provided a new guitar before the old one was even broken. It was sitting in a closet ready for me to use it. God wasn't surprised by what happened. In fact, God knew that it was going to happen. I am just thankful that on that day, I did the right thing. I listened to the Holy Spirit and gave the student a blank slate.

The student who broke the guitar was a different student after that day. I didn't have to get on them as much. They seemed kinder, and our relationship changed. The student's work was turned in on time, and the quality of the work was much better. Never underestimate the power of forgiveness and giving a blank slate.

Before we leave this subject, I want to address one more thing. Whatever happened to my brother? Well that is an amazing blank slate story in and of itself. After a few miscues here and there, my brother blossomed. He graduated college and was the first male to ever graduate from the early-childhood program at his university. He directed the university day care, and for over two decades he was a kindergarten teacher and coach. Parents would keep their children home an extra year to make sure they could get them into my brother's class. My favorite story about my brother's teaching is when he would have a student misbehave in class, he would say, "You are not going to get away with that. I invented it!"

As we close this chapter, there are a few questions we need to ask ourselves. What does it mean to give a student a blank slate? What happens when I as a teacher need a blank slate? Can you give an example of a teacher from your past who gave you a blank slate? Can you think of an example of a teacher from your past who did not give you a blank slate?

Open Door

Bear one another's burdens, and so fulfill the law of Christ.
—GALATIANS 6:2 (ESV)

I awoke one Saturday morning in extreme pain. I couldn't even roll out of bed. My stomach hurt so bad I felt like I was paralyzed. I yelled for my parents, whose room was across the hall. I just lay there on the floor of my room as my parents called the doctor. He suggested eating a whole roll of Tums and to make an appointment for Monday. The Tums helped a little, at least enough to move around, but my stomach still hurt pretty bad. Monday finally came, and after many tests and drinking what seemed like three gallons of chalk, the verdict finally came in. I had ulcers. It turns out there are consequences to stress. Who would have thought?

So why would a sixteen-year-old boy have ulcers? The short answer is because I didn't party. I was a Christian and as a junior, the starting quarterback for the football team. It was kind of a tradition at my high school that the quarterback of the football team was one of the biggest partiers in the school. I didn't fit that mold. I was propositioned almost daily to attend the alcohol parties and to submit to the peer pressure of my teammates and classmates. That pressure came from what seemed like every direction. It had reached such a high level the coaches began to notice it affecting the football team and its ability to play. The worst part was that many of the seniors were pushing to have me benched for my failure to attend parties.

Eventually the head football coach called a team meeting. All the players assembled in the only room big enough, the home economics room. I sat alone in the back of the room, ashamed and without any allies. The coach addressed the situation head-on. He looked at me and told the team that I was going to be the quarterback of this team, and if anyone didn't like it, there was the door and to turn in their equipment on the way out. I was grateful for his support, but nothing was going to ease the situation. The meeting did provide a Band-Aid to help us through the rest of the season, but I felt even more alone than I did before. My only saving grace that year was an open door.

Mr. W. was my music teacher. He had been my music teacher all through school. As I moved up in grades, so did he. He was amazing at teaching music, and our choir grew from a dozen members to sixty members. I loved music almost as much as I loved sports. But what mattered to me that year was that Mr. W. had an open door. You see, I had an independent study class with him the first hour of every day. During this hour I was supposed to be learning to play the piano. But many days that year I wasn't practicing piano. I was unloading my life to a teacher who would sit and listen and let me get stuff off my chest. I don't know what I would have done had it not been for an amazing teacher who cared more about me than me learning to play the piano.

What are your priorities in the classroom? Is it getting through the curriculum for the day? Is it preparing your students for the test? What if one of your students needed to get something off their chest or they would explode? Do you have time in the day to talk with your students? Do you have an open-door policy in your classroom? How can you put in your schedule some time to make sure you have an open door?

Integrity

*Whoever walks in integrity walks securely, but he
who makes his ways crooked will be found out.*
—PROVERBS 10:9 (ESV)

My first teaching job! I was so excited. I graduated college
in December and was thrilled to get an opportunity to jump
into teaching. It was rare to have an opening in the middle of
the school year, but God blessed me with this opportunity.
The school that hired me was your typical elementary school
in the upper Midwest.

The teacher I took over for had signed her contract
for the year but never taught that year. She was battling
cancer, and for the whole first semester, her third-grade class
had substitute teachers. Yes, it was a little chaotic in the
classroom by the time I arrived. I started in January, and I
taught math and science. Things began to settle down as we
prepared the students for the state test.

Finally, test week arrived, and like most schools,
schedules were abandoned to make sure testing was
accommodated. Of course this was a pencil-and-paper test
because it was way before computer-based tests. As I was

helping with the proctoring, I noticed that some teachers would walk by students, point to certain problems, and whisper, "You need to check that one again." They seemed to hover around the struggling students, pointing, whispering, and gesturing all through the test. The test had a time limit of forty-five minutes, but most sessions went over five to ten minutes before the teacher would collect the test booklets. I even remember walking by classrooms at lunch and seeing students still working in their test booklets. As a first-year teacher, I was too scared to say anything, afraid I might lose my job or even the opportunity for a potential job next year. So I didn't say a thing.

Time went on, and the end of the school year was at hand. The thought of state testing had long since passed from my mind. While in a staff meeting, the superintendent was excited to give the results of the state test. The results were amazing, and every student in our third grade passed the state test. My heart sank; I had a sick feeling in my stomach. As everyone congratulated the teachers on a magnificent accomplishment, in my heart I knew that it wasn't real. It was like a team cheating to win the championship. I didn't want to be a part of a team that did not play by the rules. I could not sleep that night. For fear of needing a good recommendation, I just let it go. But when offered a job by that district for the next year, I declined and moved on to another district.

We can come up with many reasons why testing may not be fair or why little Johnny or Susy should be given more time or help on the test. But at the end of the day, it is still cheating, and it is wrong. I believe God has given each of us a conscious, a place for the Holy Spirit to dwell, to lead, to prompt us, and to show us what is right and wrong. As teachers, we are the role models for our students.

When students see us helping when we shouldn't, or giving them extra time when it's not allowed, we are teaching our students that rules don't matter. I remember seeing in the news schools getting caught having pizza parties where teachers and administrators were changing answers on students' standardized tests. I probably should have done or said something that day, but I didn't. What I did do was make a vow to make sure that I would never cheat on a standardized test in my classroom.

We can't change those around us or dictate what happens in other classrooms. We can only control what happens in our classroom. So the hard question for each of us as teachers is this: Are we going to demonstrate integrity in our classroom? Are we going to abide by the rules of the state test? How will you handle it if an administrator instructs you to fudge here and there? These may seem like hard questions, but in reality, it comes back to this: Do you have integrity?

Adaptation

For though I am free from all, I have made myself a servant to all, that I might win more of them. To the Jews I became as a Jew, in order to win Jews. To those under the law I became as one under the law (though not being myself under the law) that I might win those under the law.

—1 CORINTHIANS 9:19–23 (ESV)

I love this scripture because it teaches us that we need to adapt how we present our message those receiving it. Paul did not change the message; he just adapted it to those who were hearing it. As teachers, we need to do the same thing. The curriculum does not change, but how we present that information may change from year to year based on who is in our classroom.

"What is wrong with these kids?" I asked, driving home from school. It was day 3 of my new job teaching third grade. The students were immature and illiterate. I was not sure I would make it through this semester. I was a brand-new teacher and my life had just been thrown upside down. *I'm not sure I even like third-graders. Aliens must have come and sucked their brains out!* I thought. Why did I feel this way?

I felt this way because I didn't know how to adapt to my audience.

During my student teaching and coursework at my university, I always seemed to be put in fifth and sixth grade classrooms. I had learned to relate and teach this age group really well. It never dawned on me that my training was lacking because I had never been in the younger grades. So there I was, fresh out of college and ready to take on my first teaching assignment, and I was thrown into this third-grade class. These students could barely tie their shoes, they could hardly read, and forget about having an intelligent conversation with them. I know this because I tried.

Much like Paul in Corinth, I had to learn to adapt to my audience. My audience was eight- and nine-year-olds. I needed to get their attention and somehow keep it as I was teaching. So how did I accomplish that? First, I started by bringing in my guitar. The students loved the music. I would play funny songs I learned in 4-H camp and other places. The students couldn't wait to sing the songs and laugh. Then I realized I could add curriculum to music, and this would really help to secure the teaching. So I began by putting a planets' poem I learned as a child to music, and created a planets' song. I also took a subtraction poem I found and put that to music, so now I teach subtraction using this song. Multiplication can be a hard thing to learn, so I put the eights' multiplication table to music to help the students. They absolutely loved the music, and now they were learning the curriculum at the same time. I was beginning to adapt my teaching to my audience. My curriculum did not change; I still taught space, subtraction, and multiplication. What changed was how I delivered it.

Another time really stands out where I had to adapt to my students. While student teaching, I taught a few lessons in an inner-city school with a large number of Hmong students. As I was teaching my lessons and interacting with the students, I noticed that the Hmong children would not look at or interact with me. Though I tried to engage them, they just seemed aloof. I thought that they were just disinterested in the lessons. Later, while talking to the classroom teacher, she informed me that in the Hmong culture, it was disrespectful to make eye contact with an adult. So when the Hmong students looked down and it seemed like they were not interested in my lessons, in reality, they were just being respectful like their culture expected them to be. Sometimes adaptation means we must do some research and learn new things about other cultures, disabilities, diseases, music, and languages.

In this chapter I wanted to get you thinking about how you can refine the way you deliver your message. You might have multiple cultures or languages represented in your classroom. Maybe you have special needs students in your classroom. Possibly you are teaching a different grade for the first time. What can you do, or how can you change how you deliver your message to give your students the best chance of learning? Are you willing to adapt?

Private Life Matters

A good name is to be chosen rather than great riches, and favor is better than silver or gold.
—PROVERBS 22:1-29 (ESV)

When you are a teacher, the hat never comes off. I don't care if you are in Dollar General, Walmart, or the local grocery store. It seems never to fail that while I am off trying to buy something at the store, I will run into some of my students. I love seeing them; and unfortunately, that may be the only time I see a parent. But that is another story. As teachers, we are constantly being watched.

A good friend tells of a situation where one day he was driving the school bus and had a pen in his mouth to check off the stops. The next day he was called into the bus manager's office. The manager said a call had come in, and someone had noticed he was smoking on the school bus. This man had not smoked a day in his life. He had a pen in his mouth. We need to be so careful not only in our public lives but also in our private lives. Eyes are always watching.

Over the years we have seen the drop in respect for teachers in our society. Why is that? My belief is that teachers have separated their public lives from their private lives. Today, when teachers leave the school parking lot for the day, they feel they are free to live any kind of lifestyle they want. The boundaries that once held teachers accountable are being torn down. The moral decay of our society has weaved its way into the teaching profession. So naturally, the respect that teachers once had in society has been slowly deteriorating along with society. Indiscretions that would have gotten a teacher fired Twenty years ago don't even bat an eye in today's world. The number of teachers, male and female, caught in sexual relationships with students has skyrocketed. To add insult to injury, the introduction of Facebook, Instagram, TikTok, and many other platforms has only increased the moral slide. What was once done in private is now being posted for the world to see. Many college students are finding that employers are looking at applicant's online accounts and using that information in making hiring decisions. I believe that online platforms have their place and can be used to help our profession, our school districts, and universities. But we need to be careful and make sure that our private lives reflect our public lives. If you don't believe that, I urge you to find another profession. The decline of respect for teachers is getting worse, and it won't change until we, as teachers, hold our profession to a higher standard. We started this book with a quote from James. I think it fits very nicely right here.

> Not many of you should become teachers, my brothers, for you know that we who teach will be judged with greater strictness. (James 3:1 ESV)

We need to judge ourselves more strictly than the public. I want our profession to be respected and admired for the amazing people we are, people who do extraordinary things every day! Let us finish this chapter with a few personal questions: What do your online accounts look like? If your employer had access to all your information, what would they find? Are you living two different lives? Do you act one way at school and completely different in your private life? Does your language change in the teacher's lounge compared to the classroom? Which person does little Johnny see at Dollar General?

Community

Iron sharpens iron, and one man sharpens another.
—PROVERBS 27:17 (ESV)

"Amy is ready to be a classroom teacher. Who needs help?" You will hear me say those words a lot in my classroom. I believe in students teaching students. It is a way to build community. Being a coach and a teacher for twenty-plus years, I have learned the importance of community. It really stood out to me when I moved to a different state and started teaching at a new district. The elementary school that I was now a part of received $25,000 based on the school's test scores. I was astonished. The school immediately used that money to buy technology for the students, the ones who earned it. The next year the school again received another large check based on their test scores. I quickly realized that in this state, we can win as a team or lose as a team. As a coach I understood that philosophy, so I immediately implemented a team concept in my classroom. Why? Because if we could win as a team in the classroom, there would be a prize at the end that would benefit the students. I believe this verse sums up what I am trying to get across to you.

> Two are better than one, because they have
> a good reward for their toil. For if they fall,
> one will lift up his fellow. (Ecclesiastes 4:9–
> 12 ESV)

If there is one thing I know after teaching many years, you are going to have high students, middle students, and low students. The ideal philosophy is that each group keeps moving up. When I first started teaching, most of my time was spent with the low kids trying to get them to move up. The middle got a little of my time. And the high students? Forget that; they are already good. This is possibly the worst model of teaching in the world. Yet through my experiences in many school districts, this is what happens in most classrooms. If I were to translate this philosophy to coaching a basketball team, the coach would be spending all their time with the weaker players, very little with the middle group, and none with the best players. Worst of all, the coach would never have the players working together. Not a winning formula if you are trying to win games. The coach would probably be fired after one season. Yet that is what we do as teachers. We may move one of the groups, but we never move the whole community. So how do we move the whole community?

Students Teaching Students

This is not a new concept, and I am sure you can find volumes of books that explain it much better than I can. But here's how it works in my classroom. It starts with me sharing the message that state tests matter, and how state tests affect students, schools, parents, businesses, and your neighbors down the street. In short, good schools equal higher home values. That is all part of the buy-in. Then I give the history of our school receiving $25,000 for the test scores and how that directly affected the students. Each student received a laptop to use in school. Then I bring it down to the classroom. "We win as a team and lose as a team." My students can quote that in their sleep. This whole time I have been developing a community. Each student is essential, and each student is responsible for each other.

Now comes the teaching. I begin by demonstrating the skills for that day. The "I Can" statement, notes, and examples are written in the students' notebooks. Then we practice together. After much practice, it is time for the students to demonstrate they have mastered the skill. If your classroom is like mine, only about 25 percent of the kids have gotten it at this point. So what do you do now? This is where students teaching students comes in. If we win as a team and lose as a team, it is absolutely critical to move the whole community. So instead of me trying to get to all fifteen students who didn't get it, I have five teachers who already know how to do the skill. Those five students jump in as teachers and start teaching the ones who didn't get it. The community is starting to come together. Within a short time we have enough teachers so that there is one-on-one teaching going on in the classroom. Who's benefiting? Everyone. Some days Johnny is the teacher, and other days Johnny is the student. But in all cases, everyone is getting what they need. So when we have a conversation about the "big test," we are all invested and willing to help each other achieve as a community. Because we win as a team and lose as a team.

As we close this chapter, I want you to think about community. As teachers, we tend to be more concerned with individual students. As we should be. But if a basketball coach only worried about each individual's personal skills, I doubt they would ever win a game because basketball requires individual skills and community skills to win. In the classroom we have unfortunately put all the emphasis on individual skills and less on community skills. Here are some questions to help you consider how you can incorporate community in your classroom. How are you going to handle students who are at different levels in your classroom? Do you feel community in the classroom is important and why or why not? How would you promote community in your classroom or subject area?

Special Students

Children are a gift from the Lord;
they are a reward from him.

—PSALM 127:3 (NLT)

"Mr. P., I am not doing my work. I am being naughty," That conversation always made me chuckle. One year I had a student who was blind and delayed in her education. She was very strong-willed, and because of her disability, she would just blurt out things to get my reaction or my attention. Obviously she could not see if I was paying attention, so she would verbally make sure I was.

When I went through my college training to be a teacher, one of the biggest things missing in my education was how to deal with special needs students. Unless you are majoring in special education, your instruction in and contact with special needs students is very limited. As teachers, we need to make sure that we are planning and creating ways to accommodate and include those students with special needs. Believe me, there are always going to be things you miss and need to change midstream.

Another student of mine had dwarfism. All the previous

years in school, they had a full-time nurse with them, but now that they were in third grade, they were medically well enough to not need a full-time nurse. It was going to be their first year all on their own in a classroom. I was scared to death that something was going to happen to this fragile student!

We had many accommodations for this student, like wooden steps to the drinking fountain, a different bathroom, and a smaller desk. In the classroom I had to pay close attention because when this student raised their hand, it never went above their head. Unless you were looking at the student, you would never know they were even raising their hand. In middle school, all the doors had to have a rope taped to the handles because this student got stuck one day between the inner and outer doors and could not reach the door handles. They even had a child's scooter the student would use to scoot around to classes quicker. There was a large orange flag on the back, so other students wouldn't run into her. As my principals love to say, "Monitor and adjust."

Another year we ordered a bus for our elementary field trip and didn't realize until the bus showed up that it was not handicap-equipped for one of our students in a wheelchair. One of the teachers had to drive that student in a car. It was not a huge issue, but as teachers we need to make sure that we are including and accommodating our special needs students.

Some students may have mental disabilities instead of physical ones. Sometimes I needed to have real conversations with my class on appropriate behavior and how the class could help in accommodating that student. You might be surprised how students will step up and help in those situations. Modifying work and presenting work differently are also ways to help students with special needs.

Some teachers have had many experiences with special needs children, but many have not. If you have not had much experience with special needs children, you might want to research accommodations for them. Maybe spend some time in the special education room getting to know the students. Play with them at recess, and learn to become comfortable around them.

I end this chapter with a few questions that will help us to reflect on teaching students with special needs. Do you feel equipped to have a special needs student in your room? What could you do to feel more prepared to handle a special needs student? How would you accommodate a special needs child in your room physically and educationally?

Teaching versus Facilitating

*All Scripture is breathed out by God and profitable
for teaching, for reproof, for correction, and for
training in righteousness, that the man of God may
be competent, equipped for every good work.*
—2 TIMOTHY 3:16-17 (ESV)

There is a paradigm shift in learning going on today. In fact, it started with the invention of the internet. Education has completely changed. For example, I just put a new thermostat in my Jeep a few days ago from watching a YouTube video, and it only cost me $30.00. That is a whole lot cheaper than the hundreds the dealership wanted to charge me for putting in a new one. The phrase, "Google it," has become part of everyone's vocabulary, and it is completely changing the way information is created, synthesized, and disseminated. Events happening on the other side of the world are instantly reported and can be seen in real time anywhere on the planet. With all this change in technology happening around us, it was bound to affect education as well.

I remember a conversation a few years ago with my principal about this very subject. My point to her was simple. The old paradigm of a teacher lecturing and controlling all the information a student gets is completely outdated for many reasons. First is the fact that the information the teacher is disseminating may be outdated. If the teacher is still using their notes from ten years ago, they are probably outdated, and that teacher needs to upgrade anyway. Second is that students can jump on any computer and find just about any information they need. I had a student taking a test at home, and they googled and found the exact test with all the answers.

With the explosion of technology in our world, students have more access to information and any library. That was the point I was making to my principal. It really doesn't matter where they learn it, how they learn it, or who they learn it from as long as they learn it.

Many teachers feel they are losing control of the information they teach because of unlimited access to information. Some teachers don't want their students to have the ability to seek information on their own for many reasons. What if the information is bad? What if the information is inappropriate for their age? How can we filter what they see and hear? All these are valid, and many districts have spent thousands of dollars trying to answer these questions.

Being a fourth-grade math teacher, I have run into this very problem. With COVID-19 happening in our world, most districts have turned to some type of virtual learning. With virtual learning comes the loss of direct control as a teacher. During my division unit, I spent many hours creating videos on how to divide using long division. What did my virtual learners do? The virtual learners pulled up the calculator or used Google to find the answer to the division problem. How did I know? They didn't show their work, and they had a decimal instead of a remainder. They didn't even take time to watch the learning videos I created. So as a teacher, am I grading the process, or am I grading the product of learning? And in the big scheme of life, when those students are twenty-five years old, aren't they going to pull up the calculator anyway? Regardless of how we feel about it, education is changing, and we need to figure out how we are going to educate the next generation. I believe the teachers' job description is beginning to change into being a facilitator and less of a teacher.

So what does facilitating look like? Instead of *being* the encyclopedia, we teach them how to *use* the encyclopedia. Of course the encyclopedia has been replaced to some extent by Google, YouTube, Alexa, Siri, and a whole host of online technologies, websites, and apps. With so many avenues for students to travel, teachers must help them to navigate and explore safely the world or technology. Our job has shifted from disseminating information to teaching the students what information is correct, useful, and, of course, how to use it. We still have state standards and curriculum that must be addressed, but now we are addressing them differently.

In fourth-grade math I may assign a Khan Academy lesson or create a video for the students to watch. There are multiple platforms that I can use to teach my students. My students can now access that information anytime they want to and from wherever they want. It doesn't have to only be from 9:00–10:00 Monday through Friday in Mr. P.'s classroom. With access to so many teaching tools, I have students turning in assignments all day long and even from other classes because they had finished their work early in that class. I have students teaching and helping other students in other classes. I have become more of a facilitator, directing students instead of just dictating from the front of the classroom.

This chapter has brought up some very difficult questions and ideas about how the next generations of students are going to learn. I think it will be harder before it gets easier because technology is moving faster than the educational paradigm. Our closing questions are very difficult to answer. What do you think education will look like in ten or twenty years? Do you see yourself as a teacher or a facilitator? What role does technology have in the classroom? How do you control and protect students when using technology for learning? How do you control or facilitate learning from home?

Data Doesn't Lie

"I am failing my students," I said. I had just received my copy of the STAR reading scores for my third-grade class. It was my second year teaching, and I thought I was doing a pretty good job. They were passing my class, so everything was great, right? Not according to the STAR reading test, with sarcasm.

My school, along with many others, jumped on the, "You have to have data," bandwagon. It was a large paradigm shift in education, and it would expose many areas of weakness in classrooms and districts. Well it had completely exposed my poor teaching in reading and left me feeling ashamed and embarrassed. I was so embarrassed that I decided to return to college and get my master's in reading. I was going to fix this reading problem one way or another. So off to college I went to get my master's degree in reading.

The reason I share about that dark time in my teaching career is because teachers have a tendency not to be aware of the weaknesses in their teaching. Students may not do well on certain units or areas, and teachers tend to chalk it up to many things. Excuses could be things like a low class or a rough home life; there is a whole laundry list of excuses. The last thing a teacher looks at is the fact that they might not be doing a good job teaching their students.

Data is one of those things teachers tend to cringe at. The fear of getting the results of the state standardized test literally paralyzes many teachers. I remember one of my first years teaching the results of the state test for our school district came back in July. A couple weeks later, every teacher received an email basically saying they were doing a terrible job! Nothing motivates you more than an email stating you did a terrible job two weeks before school starts.

Data is not going away. Over the years I have learned that instead of resisting and fearing data, I can take advantage of it, and let it drive my teaching. Believe it or not, I am the one calling my administrator all summer long, asking if the state test results have come in yet. Why? I want to know how my kids did. What areas did they struggle with? Did I reach my goal on the number of students who passed it? How many students made it into the advanced category? Who didn't pass, and what areas did they fail? You see, all these questions start to drive my teaching for the next year. If I have a low area across the board, then I need to address that area better next year. Data becomes my friend instead of an enemy.

So the more data we have to work with, the more informed we are, and that information can drive our teaching. I use a few forms of data in my classroom. I begin the year with immediately taking the STAR math test. I have the students take it five times, at the beginning of the year and after each quarter. The STAR math test will locate low and troubled areas of the students coming in, and I can address those areas as I teach the grade-level curriculum.

I also keep track of basic facts for each of my students. I continue to track those throughout the school year as well. Basic facts, especially multiplication facts, are critical for fourth-grade students. Just about everything we do in fourth grade is based on multiplication facts, so that is an essential skill for my students. My goal is that all fourth-graders can do one hundred multiplication facts in five minutes.

Our school also contracts with the ACT Aspire Interim tests two times a year. We take it once in the fall and then in the winter. It prepares the students for taking the ACT Aspire, which is our state test. The test is basically the same test with different questions and allows you to see growth in each student. It also allows you to see areas in which your curriculum is lacking.

The final data point that I use is the daily assignments and tests. This year I have tried something that I have never done before, and I feel it reaped great benefits. I graded every assignment this year. That may seem impossible, but I was able to do it all in the classroom and not take work home to grade. I would have the students turn in their homework as they walked into the classroom. While the students did XtraMath (a math fact program on the computer), I corrected the assignments. It took me about five to ten minutes to correct them. The students would finish about the time I finished, and I would hand the assignments back. We would have "RTI" time, which is when the students would correct or fix their assignments and get the extra help they needed for that assignment.

Correcting every assignment means lots of data. Last quarter I graded twenty-five assignments. But students can hide under the radar in classrooms where very little data is collected. Teachers who don't collect data don't really know where their students are. And by the time they do, it may be too late. This process allowed me to really get to know my students, their tendencies, and to put in a plan of action to fix the issues that arose.

When we start to embrace data and use data to drive instruction, we will start to see huge growth in our students. I can't wait for the STAR results or the ACT Aspire results throughout the year because it gives me an opportunity to show the success of each student. I enjoy walking into my administrator's office with my test results so I can brag on my students!

There is one more thing we need to address before we leave this chapter on data. We must allow the students to be part of the data. At least for me. In the past I would just keep the results to myself, good or bad. The students had no stake in the test because they were not going to see the results anyway. There was no incentive for them to do well, and many times they didn't do well just for that reason. Then I started to share the STAR test results with each student. I called each student to my desk, and we went over the results. What the student scored didn't matter. We would set a goal and make a plan to reach that goal on the next test. Now when my students take the test again, they have a goal and a buy-in, so they put more effort into taking the tests. The students are excited to see their results and want to share them with their parents.

Data can be an enemy or a friend. In closing this chapter, we need to ask ourselves which one of these is data to us? Do we cringe when the word "data" is brought up? Or are we excited to see and share our data with all stakeholders? How can we use data to drive our teaching? How can we get students to be part of the data collection so there is a buy-in?

Getting Students to Remember

You shall teach them to your children, talking of them when you are sitting in your house, and when you are walking by the way, and when you lie down, and when you rise. You shall write them on the doorposts of your house and on your gates.

—DEUTERONOMY 11:19–20

Yup, that was definitely a big fat F on my paper. Reader, you are reading a book written by a man who went to college and barely passed composition class. My first paper in college was that big fat F. I quickly learned that I needed some serious help in the writing department. My professor was gracious enough to allow me to bring my paper in a week before it was due to help me with it. By the time we went over it a couple times, it would end up being a B. I could live with that.

While in college getting a master's degree in reading, I soon realized that I would have to write a thesis to graduate. But there is one major problem with that: I can't write! My professors were great and walked me through the process of writing my thesis, and yes, I did graduate. I bring all that up for this reason: That thesis changed my teaching life.

The cohort I was part of was instructed to write a thesis on something that was really important to our teaching. Find that area you really needed help with or an area that you are passionate about. I was teaching third grade at the time, and my students struggled with memorizing. They couldn't remember their math facts, spelling words, vocabulary words, and science and social studies vocabularies. It was like I was talking to a wall. I wished there was a way to open the top of my students' heads and just dump the information in. Since that was not an option, I decided that I should write my thesis on how I could get my students to remember.

As I poured over the information—which there is a ton of, by the way—I soon realized once again that I was lacking in the teaching department. There were lots of ways for teachers to improve memorization in the classroom. Why wasn't I taught any of this in my bachelor program? Seriously, this information would later turn me into the teacher I am today! So let's look at a few of the things I learned and implemented from my thesis.

Notebooks

The most important thing I learned in researching memory is the need to use a notebook. Research showed that when a student would hear, see, and write information, they would have a much better chance of remembering that information. I took that information and ran with it. I made notebooks for math, science, social studies, and writing. I had the students take notes every day. We start each class with writing our, "I can," statement in our notebooks for that day.

When I was teaching third grade, every one of my students were taking notes in every class. I would make notebooks for science and social studies. I fold a twelve-inch by eighteen-inch piece of construction paper in half and put five lined pieces of paper and five pieces of copy paper for pictures and diagrams inside. Then I stapled it. As I wrote the notes or diagrams on the board, the students wrote them in their notebooks. It took a while to train them on good note-taking, but the benefits were fabulous.

I always allowed them to use the notebooks for assignments and tests. That gave them a huge incentive to take good notes. Let me tell you that I have never stopped using notebooks in all my classes for the last nineteen years of teaching. My test scores have been great because of them. I feel most teachers underestimate the power and importance of notebooks in the classroom.

Music

I have already talked about this, but let me just reiterate the importance of music in the classroom. Besides writing songs for curriculum and memorization, I believe that music in the background also helps the brain when it comes to math. That was another research nugget I gleaned and immediately put into practice in my classroom. I play Bach, Beethoven, and many other classical artists during my math classes to help facilitate the students' learning. Music is essential, and my goal here is to challenge you as a teacher to incorporate music into your classroom if you are not already doing so.

Mnemonic Devices

A mnemonic device is anything that helps a student to remember information. An example would be the acronym HOMES. I learned that in my geography class in college and have never forgotten it. What does HOMES stand for? The Great Lakes: Lake Huron, Lake Ontario, Lake Michigan, Lake Erie, and Lake Superior. As teachers we can help students develop and create creative ways to learn the information we are teaching. I made one up a month ago in my math class. Some of my students could not remember how to multiply two-digit by two-numbers. So while driving the school bus home (I also drive the school bus), I was thinking of a way to help them. I came up with this little poem:

> Dino facing left,
> dino facing right.
> Three rows of numbers
> lets me know it's right.

The dino is a dinosaur head drawn over the multiplication pattern for the ones and tens. The mistakes the students would make was to multiply up and down and have one row of numbers. This poem helped them to remember to have three rows of numbers when multiplying. Did it work? Absolutely. I have cut in half the number of students making that multiplying error.

There are no right or wrong mnemonic devices when it comes to helping students. I make stuff up all the time to help them. Be creative, and allow yourself to just go with it. Many teachers are scared to try things because it was not done that way when they were taught, or that method is not in their curriculum books. Don't worry, there are no mnemonic police patrolling your hallways. Have the students come up with the devices if you are stumped. Some of my best ones came from students.

Getting information into the students' heads can come in many forms. Sometimes we just have to think outside the box. It may be for just that one student, but to that one student, it changes their world. Wrapping up this chapter, let's take a look at a few questions. What are some changes you can make to help your students remember? How can you use notebooks in your teaching? What mnemonic devices can you take advantage of to help your students learn? How can music play a role in your classroom?

Teaching with
COVID-19

Fear not, for I am with you; be not dismayed, for I am your God; I will strengthen you, I will help you, I will uphold you with my righteous right hand.

—ISAIAH 41:10 (ESV)

Will 2020 ever be over? I am not sure when you are reading this book, but I had to put a chapter in here about teaching with COVID-19. Not that I have any answers because right now we are in the middle of the pandemic, and no one seems to know what to do. Districts have handled COVID-19 in different ways. Some have gone completely virtual, some blended, and other schools have tried to remain open and continue teaching face-to-face. The district that I am a part of did a type of mirroring instruction. That is, we had virtual students and in-class students getting the same instruction via recorded lessons.

After the first semester of teaching with COVID-19, we do have some results. First, for most students, virtual learning is a bust. The number of students failing the first semester is unbelievably high. Second, most teachers are not prepared to teach in this new virtual era of education. In my experience, I started with eleven virtual students, and nine of them failed. That's nearly 90 percent just in my grade.

What were the reasons for the failure? No parent supervision, lack of accountability, lack of motivation, and technology issues are just a few of the problems that led to student failure. Because of the failure rate, I am happy to say that most of those students are back to face-to-face instruction and doing much better. Why would we think a child of nine or ten would have the perseverance and work ethic of an adult? Without any way to control or monitor what the child is doing during the day, teachers were left completely helpless. For those students who did succeed virtually, it was because they had a parent monitoring the instruction and homework.

There are so many questions that need to be answered, but we just don't have those answers. But I think the COVID-19 pandemic has shined a spotlight on some things that needed to be exposed. I am not sure what the answers are, but we need to ask them anyway. What can we do to make virtual learning more successful? I don't think virtual learning is going away. How do we get teachers and staff trained to teach virtually? Are the universities preparing future teachers for this new change in education? How do we teach face-to-face safely? How do you prioritize teacher and student health with student learning? If students fail, do we keep them in the same grade since they didn't learn the skills? Do we force failing students back to face-to-face instruction? I'm sure we could fill page after page of questions about how to handle teaching in this new world of pandemics. But let me end this chapter with some hope. I started this chapter with Isaiah 41:10, and it seems appropriate that we finish with it.

> Fear not, for I am with you; be not dismayed, for I am your God; I will strengthen you, I will help you, I will uphold you with my righteous right hand.

Conclusion

Do not be anxious about anything, but in everything by prayer and supplication with thanksgiving let your requests be made known to God. And the peace of God, which surpasses all understanding, will guard your hearts and your minds in Christ Jesus.

—PHILIPPIANS 4:6–7 (ESV)

You have made it through to the end. I concluded with this verse because the world today is challenging, and education has been flipped on its head. We do not know what tomorrow will bring, so we must rely on our faith. We can only do our best and leave the rest up to God. I hope that this book has helped you to step back and take a look at your teaching practices. Maybe there was a nugget here or there you could pull. Possibly an idea you can implement or a thought that caused you to want to change the way you teach. Either way, I hope you build relationships with those you work with and with those you teach. Because in the end, it is never about the information; it is about the relationship!

God bless,

Mr. P,

Printed in the United States
by Baker & Taylor Publisher Services